the art of Vivan Sundaram

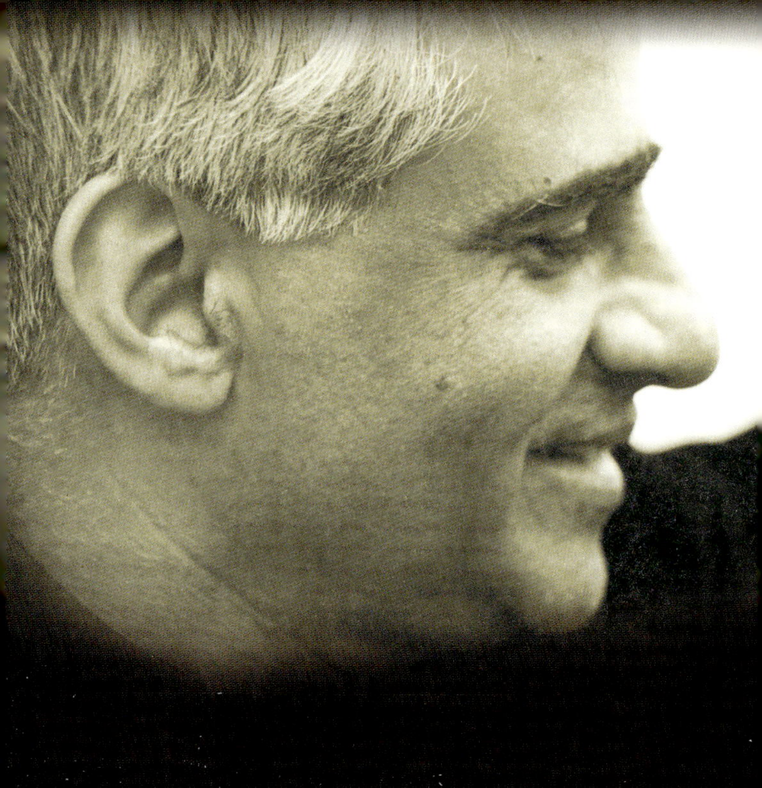

the art of

Kamala Kapoor

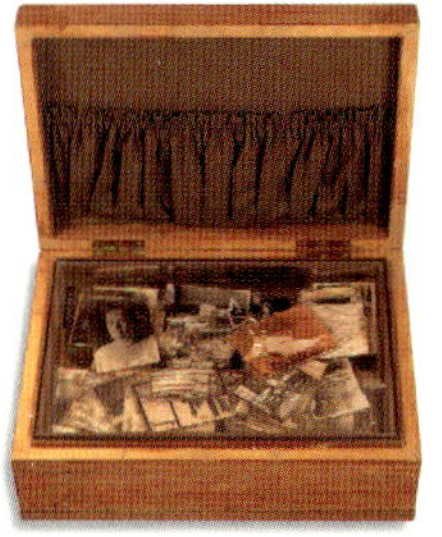

Vivan Sundaram

Lustre Press
Roli Books

As an artist, Vivan Sundaram has developed a complex sensibility: on the one side is the undeniable influence of contemporary internationalism, and on the other his own cultural memory with its non-linear heterogeneity of sources and experiences, and its ability to recast itself in modern times.

His numerous and diverse creations seem to have travelled widely in time and space, visiting assorted trends and influences, revisiting family and childhood, friends and relationships, and replenishing convictions and deeply thought-out ideologies, while remaining alert to new political realities in an ever-changing world.

Sundaram was born in Shimla in 1943. His paternal line traces its roots to south India. His Tamilian father (p.25) was an ICS officer, the second Chief Election Commissioner in post-Independence India, while his mother's side reveals his Sikh-Hungarian origins. His maternal grandfather, Sardar Umrao Singh Sher-Gil, was a scholar and an aesthete. As a more than dilettante photographer, Umrao

Singh's prolific photographs of his family included those of the legendary painter, his non-conformist daughter, Amrita Sher-Gil, Sundaram's aunt who was to die prematurely at 28; his other daughter, Indira, Sundaram's mother; Marie Antoinette; his Hungarian wife, the artist's grandmother, who would eventually take her own life; and Umrao Singh himself in quixotic poses and costumes.

While it is tempting to speculate on the development of Sundaram as an artist born to a certain inherited pre-disposition towards art, there seems to have been no fait accompli in his

The artist with his wife, Geeta Kapur

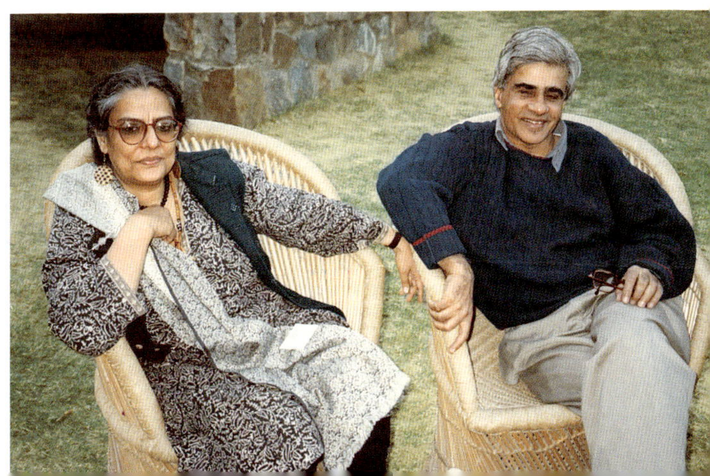

choice of art as a profession. In 1960, when he was at Doon School, his physics tutor urged him to take up art when he saw some paintings Sundaram had done at the age of 12. That led Sundaram to Rathin Mitra, the art master.

In 1961, at the suggestion of family friends, the art critic Charles Fabri, and art historian Karl Khandalavala, Sundaram joined the four-year B.A. course at the Faculty of Fine Arts in Baroda. 'I took to it immediately,' he remembers. Though his parents wanted him to study commercial art, Gulammohammed Sheikh, his 'Story of Art' teacher, and later his close friend, insisted it had to be painting.

He came into contact with Jeram Patel and Himmat Shah, and had an enduring friendship with Bhupen Khakhar, who had joined the faculty in 1962 to pursue his master's degree. K.G. Subramanyan, professor of painting at the faculty, provided Sundaram with a self-conscious approach to making art, and later became his mentor in various art projects.

It is likely that the Baroda experience

exteriorised in some ways a break with the past. It certainly instigated the emergence of certain convictions and nurtured a certain growth based on a culture of interaction and discourse, formative influences and camaraderie. A subjective questioning of his class culture had also begun to take place.

This became more visible during his stay in London from 1966 to 1970. After a post-graduation in painting at the Slade School of Art, Sundaram did a one-year course on the history of cinema. Here began a four-year long hiatus from painting. Confronted with Enoch Powel's raging racism and the horrifying reality of the Vietnam War, a political awareness began to permeate the artist's consciousness. 'I took part in almost every political demonstration at the height of the Vietnam War,' says the artist.

Back in Delhi by 1970, he returned to the art scene immediately – though not yet to making art – and became the secretary of the artists' protest against the Lalit Kala Akademi, started by Sheikh and spearheaded by Swaminathan.

Politically, this was the time that he came close to students from the Jawaharlal Nehru University as well as young CPI(M) comrades. It was finally in '72, with the drawing series, based on a poem of epic proportions and political polemic: *The Heights of Macchu Picchu,* by the Latin American poet Pablo Neruda, that Sundaram began drawing and painting again. In the same year, he organised a retrospective of Amrita Sher-Gil's paintings, did a book on her with Marg Publications, and edited her letters.

Amrita Sher-Gil died two years before Sundaram's birth. Yet she continues to live on in his work. In the oil on canvas *The Sher-Gil Family* (p. 27), a late afternoon light filters across the living room, where the family is captured as if in a theatrical tableaux, each member in a telling pose. In the foreground, Amrita turns around from her easel, her gaze locking spellbindingly with the viewer's.

With the haunting exhibition The Sher-Gil Archive, in 1995 (p. 53), an installation comprising a selection of family photographs by

Umrao Singh (described earlier), letters written by Amrita, and assorted memorabilia, the artist threaded his way back into the family labyrinth again, as if in a rite of passage, presenting the personal with the historical and archival, in an atypical gallery arrangement.

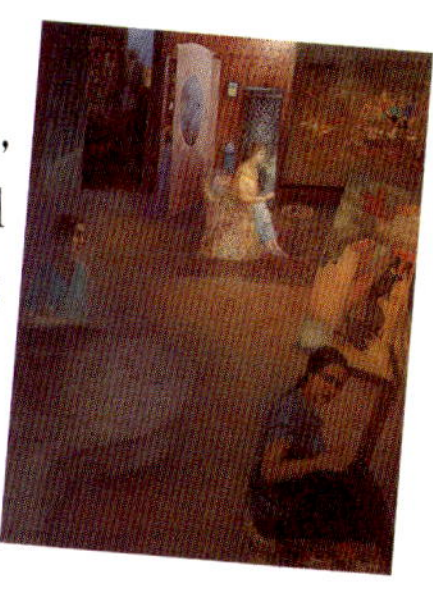

The Sher-Gil Family

'Thirty years later I'm on the same terrain,' says Sundaram. 'The letters of Amrita, with an equal length of text and images, will come out after a year. On the creative front, for the third time, the Sher-Gil family enters the frame, this time with digitally transformed photographic images.' The series, his most recent work, is called Retake of the Sher-Gil Archive: Stills from 'Amrita'.

It was in Delhi in 1966 that Sundaram met Geeta Kapur (a well-known art critic, curator, and author), whom he describes as his companion – they married much later in 1985. 'I have known her as long as my professional

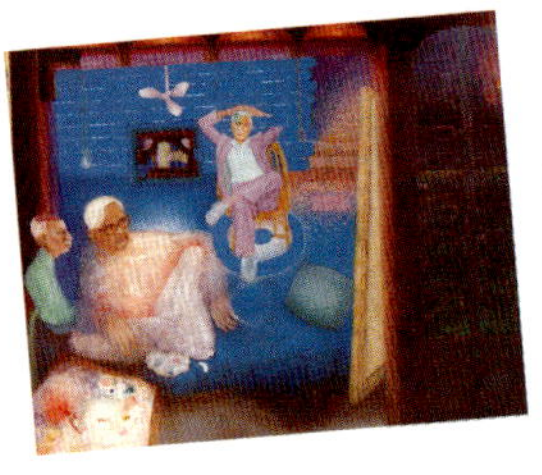

People Come and Go

creative life,' he says. They have collaborated on many art projects over the years; both are founder-members of the Kasauli Art Centre and the *Journal of Arts and Ideas*.

Sundaram, who lives and works in Delhi, is a cultural activist: he is a trustee and associate of SAHMAT (Safdar Hashmi Memorial Trust founded in 1989), an organisation that works for secularism through a cultural manifesto. He has also been a curator and an organiser of numerous artists' (and multi-disciplinary) workshops and camps for several decades.

Sundaram, as if 'homesick', had returned to live in Baroda between 1972 to 1984, and had shared living and working space with Khakhar during the early years. The painting *People Come and Go* (p. 23), featuring Khakhar in his studio, was derived from there. The work was shown in the seminal exhibition, Place for People, held in Mumbai and Delhi in 1981. Also shown at the exhibition was *Guddo* (p. 21), a response to the

Mathura rape case in '64, that involved police atrocities, and had become a burning issue.

With an uncompromising talent, and subjectively loaded canvases like *Two Boys Sitting on the Outer Wall* (p. 17) and *Big Shanti* (p. 19), both of which are allegorical/realistic representations depicting his political concerns, the artist is part of the generation that came to be known as the Baroda Group. Sundaram's figural and narrative paintings, often quotational, depicted an image-world charged with a sort of mythic energy, as if an obsessive inner vision had somehow been captured in paint (*Quintal of Grass,* cover). His themes, ranging from the socially topical to the historically personal, were invariably drawn from his own experiences and ideologies, even as they affirmed their own Indian identity (*Arabesque,* p. 29).

Over the years, Sundaram kept drawing almost as prolifically as he painted. Working on paper with all the immediacy of drawing, staining, and mark-making made for a certain sense of release, a freedom to push the frame, so to speak, that had less to do with formalist composition, and more with visual metaphor (*Orientalist*, p. 31, and *Chinese Junk and Dreaming Seamen*, p. 33). It also accommodated a new articulation, a new layering of meaning, resulting in the start of a gradual easing out of the human figure.

Moved by a visit to Birkeneau and Auschwitz, he created the exhibitions Long Night in 1988, followed by Engine Oil and Charcoal: Works on Paper, in 1991–92, a direct reference to the Gulf War, which had triggered the theme. Both works were preoccupations with war, death, and destruction, with premonitory indices of a nuclear holocaust.

There was no abrupt switch to the sculpture/installation work he became better known for from the early '90s. More in the nature of a conscious transition that had to be worked through, he began setting up strategies that went on to transfer content to discourse. Undaunted by the complexities of the issues involved in his work, or by the varieties of mediums and modalities he had taken on, he started presenting works that explored the relationship between image and idea, and structure and sensation, in unique ways.

First among these was the large multimedia exhibition called Collaboration/Combines (*Sailboat and Oar Resting Against Tent,* p. 13, and *Stone Column Enclosing the Gaze,* p. 15), held in Delhi and Mumbai in 1992. It marked the transition in his work from the two-dimensional to the three, to the emergence of the sculptural form that was compositionally and spatially more complex.

A collaboration with architects, craftsmen, photographers, and other artists became an

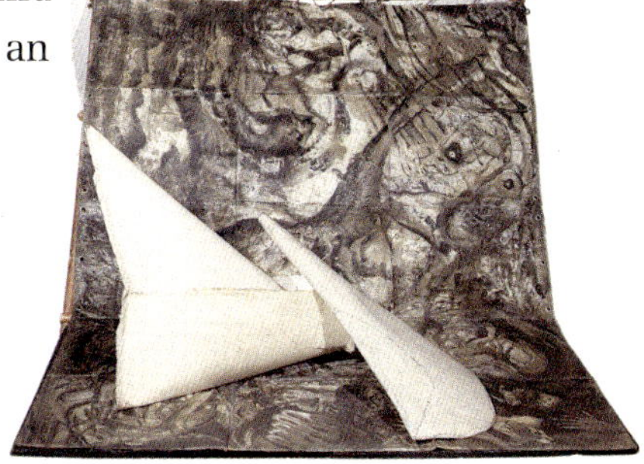

Sailboat and Oar Resting against Tent, 1992, engine oil and charcoal, stitched handmade paper and wood; drawing done by students of the Faculty of Fine Arts

ongoing practice. This was a threshold moment in the artist's life. Having reached a point of saturation in his painting, he gave it up.

Sundaram has always been interested in new materials and technologies and investigating how they can be integrated with his invented forms. As such, an important feature in several of his installations *(Carrier*, p. 59; *House/Boat*, p. 43; *Structures of Memory*) has been the use of sound and the moving image (video). With the use of interactive multimedia technology in his most recent series, Retake of the Sher-Gil Archive: Stills from 'Amrita', he seems to be extending his old fascination with multi-layered images, meanings, and dualities into new areas; exploring among other things, the play/tension between the real (photographic) and the virtual (digital image).

Avant-garde as his works are, his multimedia approach reworks themes that once spanned his canvases. It is the kind of continuity that has been emblematic of the way he has found renewal and regeneration within his own art at critical points in his career. 'I find a great deal of my art of the '90s reconstitutes through new structures and materials, a content that engages with the personal and political,' says the artist.

In the last decade, Sundaram has welded, hacksawed, photocopied, stained, video-filmed, assemblaged his materials and technique towards a focussed intention, the results being thrown open to associative processes. The levels of meanings can be re-shuffled to form complex layers, with the composite images becoming a point of departure, yet his art, suffused with history and experience, seldom relinquishes its original goal.

Even when his themes are explicitly political, as in *Memorial* (p. 47), a response to the communal riots in Mumbai after the demolition of the Babri Masjid; in *House/Boat* (p. 43), that deals with migration, dislocation, and civic collapse; or in *Structures of Memory* (conceived in

Stone Column Enclosing the Gaze: 1992, sandstone, acrylic sheet, photograph, mirror and enamel

1998, for the domed interior of the Victoria Memorial, Calcutta), based on issues of colonialism and post-colonial identity, his work dwells in the interstices between sensibility and intelligence, and radical strategies of resistance.

Along with *Black Boat,* which encoded ecological/environmental readings, the more allegorical *The Table is Laid* (p. 57) and *Carrier* (p. 59), the deeply personal *Bunk Bed* (p. 63), and the two versions of *The Sher-Gil Archive* (pp. 53, 55), most of Sundaram's works, suggesting rupture and re-alignment, have always taken place as something like 'mediations'. Else, they suggest 'interventions' – attempts to subvert social hierarchies, communal mindsets, gender and caste discriminations, political and economic disparities, as well as established genres and entrenched visual habits. In the consequent dissolution of boundaries, the experience of the art work takes place without any absolute definitions, becoming in itself challenging at a contextual and formal level, as well as open-ended in its series of possibilities.

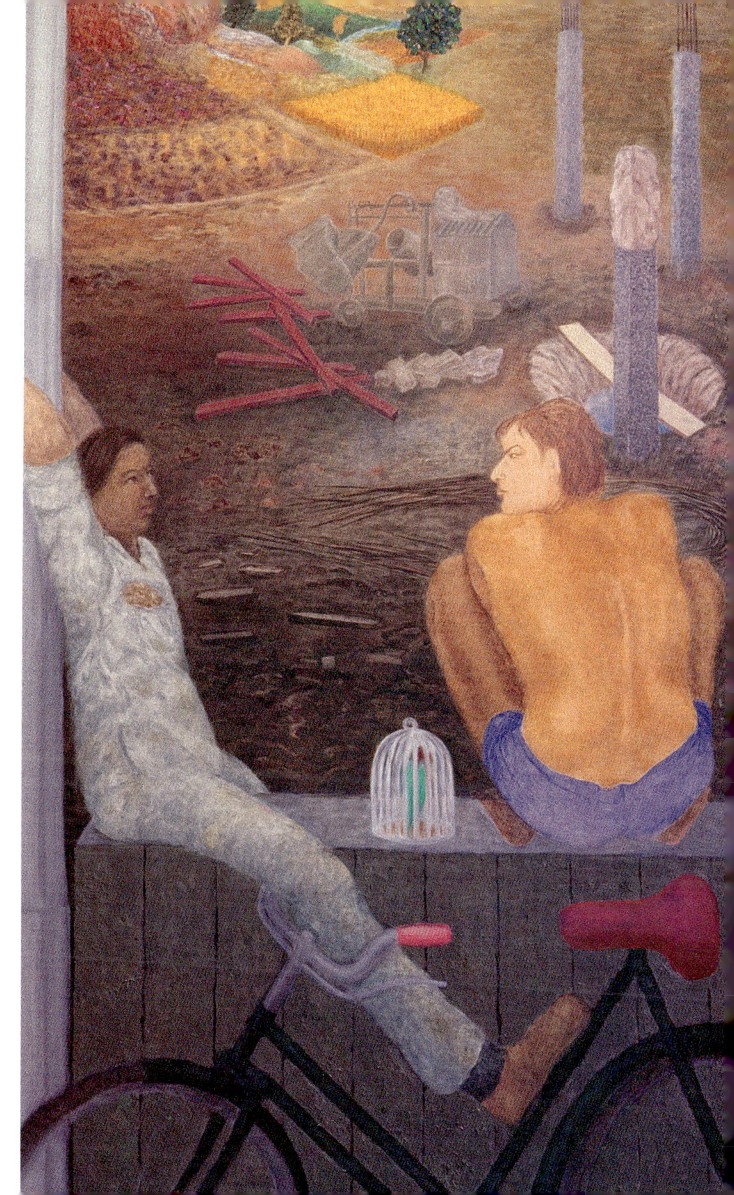

■ Vivan Sundaram, *Two Boys Sitting on the Outer Wall (Kalidas and Pandu)*, 1985
200 x 112 cm, oil on canvas, collection: Sunita Paul, New Delhi

'I start with a life situation . . . but the documentation is only up to a point . . . . My interest then moves to the figures acquiring a certain iconic presence . . . . They become as if carriers or agents . . . through them we move on to other worlds.' (Vivan Sundaram in an interview in 1986 at Mumbai)

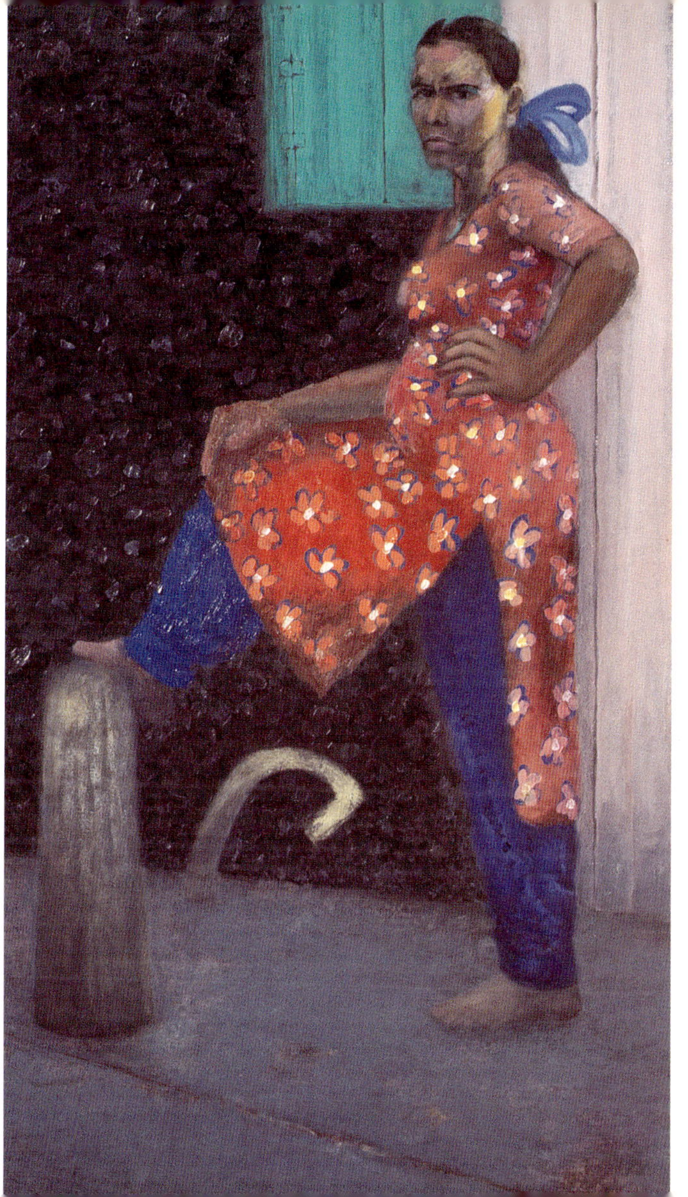

■ Vivan Sundaram, *Big Shanti*, 1982-85

200 x 110 cm, oil on canvas, collection: Mira Nair, New York

Here, the bold body language of the woman exudes pent-up anger and bitter strength. Unlike the still forms in some of the artist's other works, this one resonates with feeling and aggressive visuality. The colours show little of their usual tonal nuances and textural treatment, as the backgrounds and atmosphere give way to a close-up portrait of the powerful mother figure, also seen in the far distance in Guddo, *an earlier canvas.*

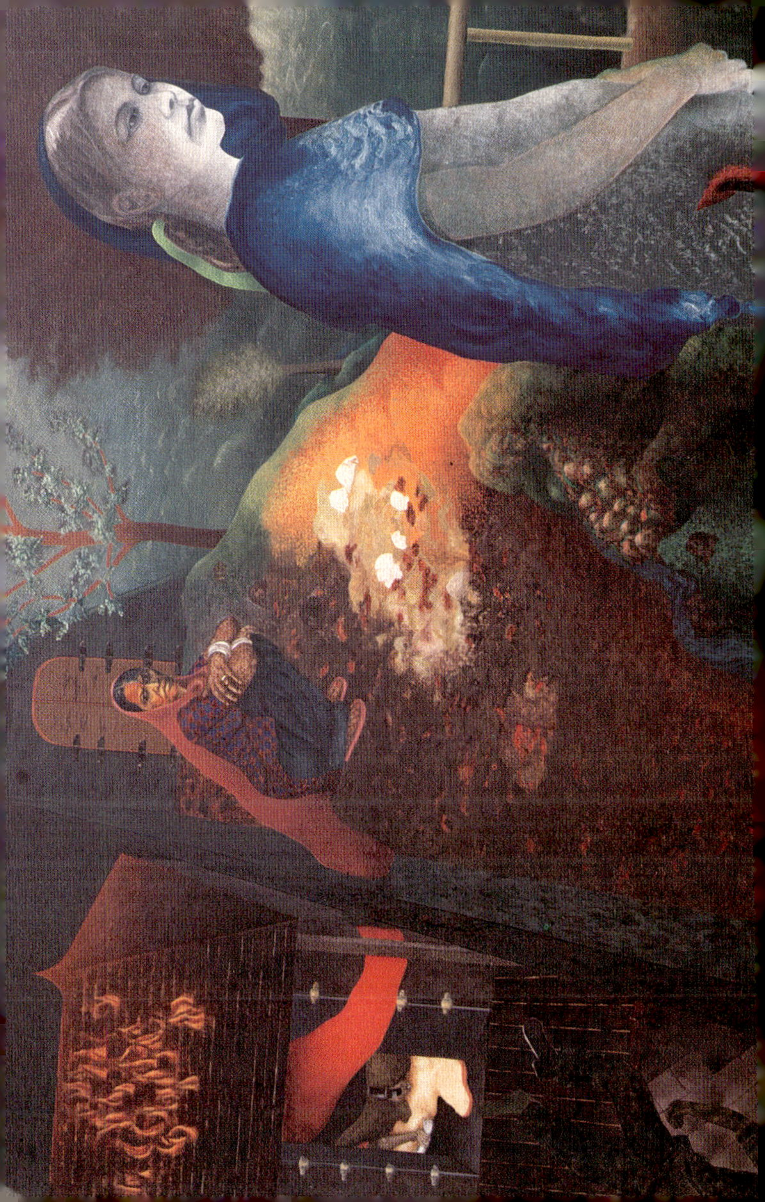

■ Vivan Sundaram, *Guddo,* 1980

112 x 137 cm, oil on canvas, collection: Roopankar Museum of Fine Art, Bhopal

The Western quotation is visible in the da Vinci-like treatment of the landscape behind the ethereal-looking young girl. References like these blend effortlessly with the archetypal elements of Indian miniature painting, as in the use of luminous colour, in the enlargement and diminishing of figures, in the bending of spatial norms, and in the use of nearness and distancing for narrative sequencing.

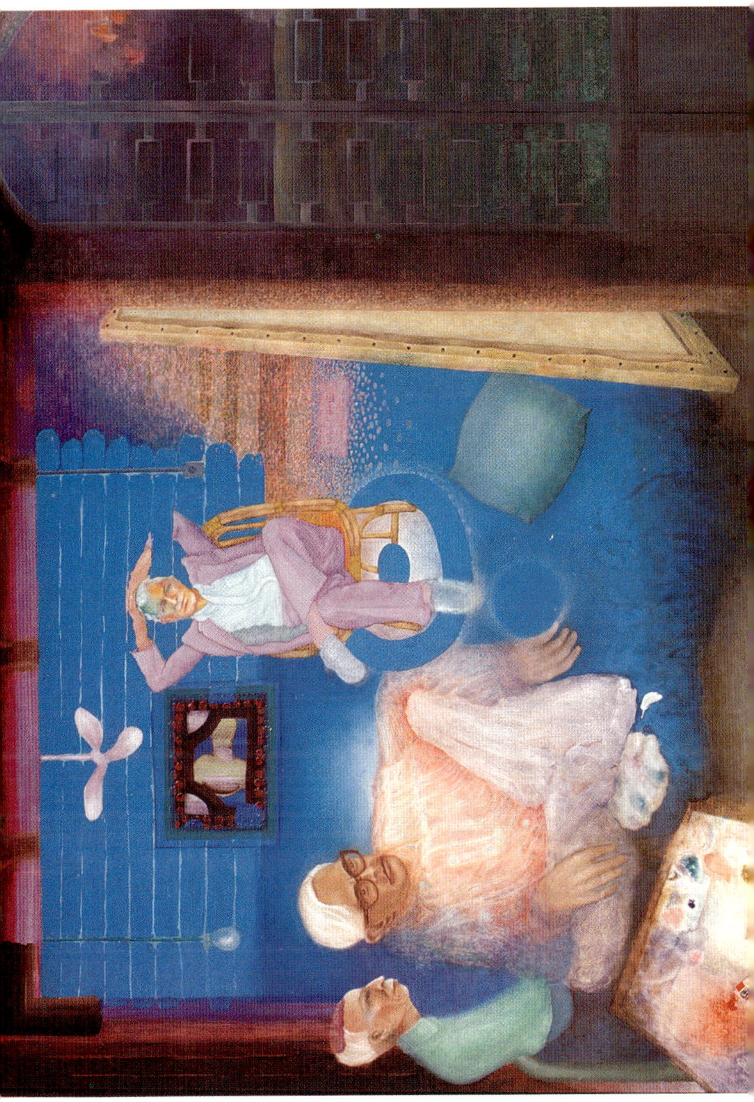

■ Vivan Sundaram, *People Come and Go*, 1981

123 x 154 cm, oil on canvas, 1981, collection: Jyoti Limited, Baroda

The placement of the three figures, the artist Bhupen Khakhar, his friend Vallabhbhai, and the British artist Howard Hodgkin, recalls the manner in which a film camera would break up a scene in a mid-shot, a close-shot and a close-up, so as to draw attention to a particular person or detail. At the same time the images, even the inanimate ones, are manipulated not for any pictorial syntheses, but for playing out the various interactive possibilities generated by their combinations.

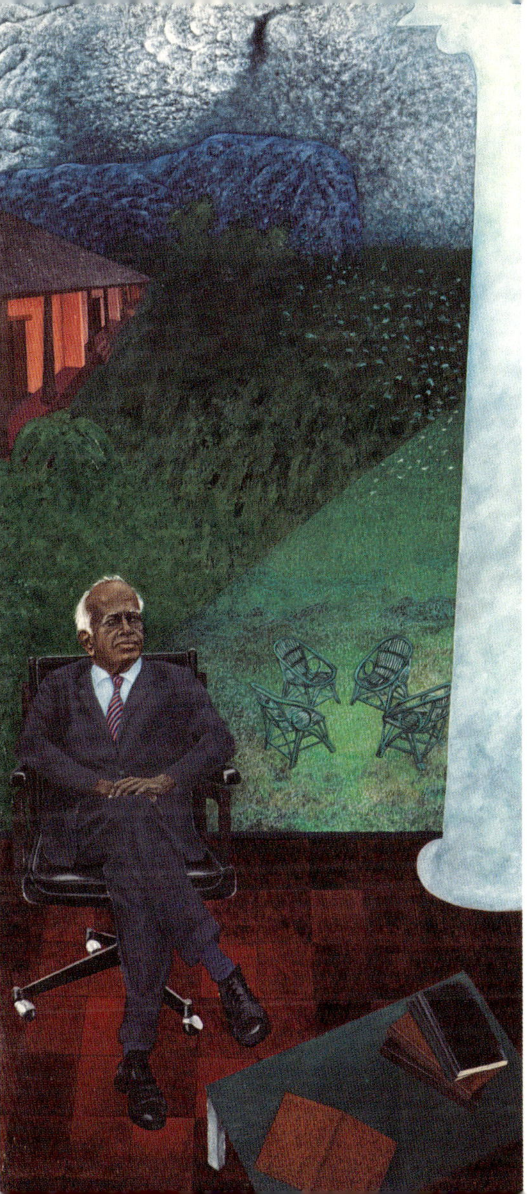

■ Vivan Sundaram, *Portrait of Father*, 1980

183 x 84 cm, oil on canvas, collection: National Gallery of Modern Art, New Delhi

'I have painted my father [the painting is about a particular person and is photographically realistic] . . . . It is also about painting a certain period, a certain era . . . I see painting as a process. The evolution, however, is not sequential or linear, but more in the form of a spiral. This gets related to the subject matter, which attempts to deal with a very large spectrum, from the personal/autobiographical to the socio-political.' (Vivan Sundaram in an interview in 1986 at Mumbai)

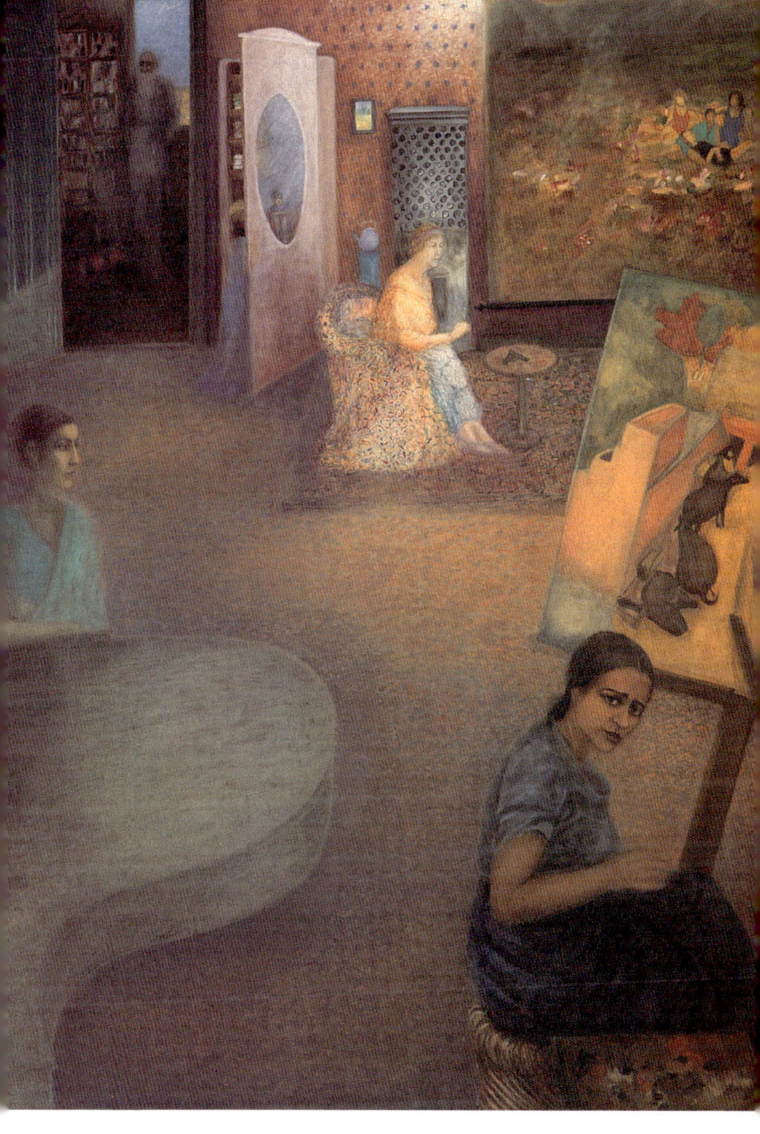

■ Vivan Sundaram, *The Sher-Gil Family*, 1983–84

229 x 175 cm, oil on canvas, collection: Artist, New Delhi

'The painting is a reconstruction . . . . What interested me was the aspect of locating the self in the world, though not in any narcissistic, self-centred manner . . . . One way of particularising this was to start with people nearest to you . . . . In the seeming order, there is a sense of sudden disorder . . . as if a collapse were imminent . . . as if the light is about to go out . . . . It is based around 1946; and there are links to colonial India . . . . It also has a European connection, a Chekhovian aspect to it.' (Vivan Sundaram, in the 1986 Mumbai interview)

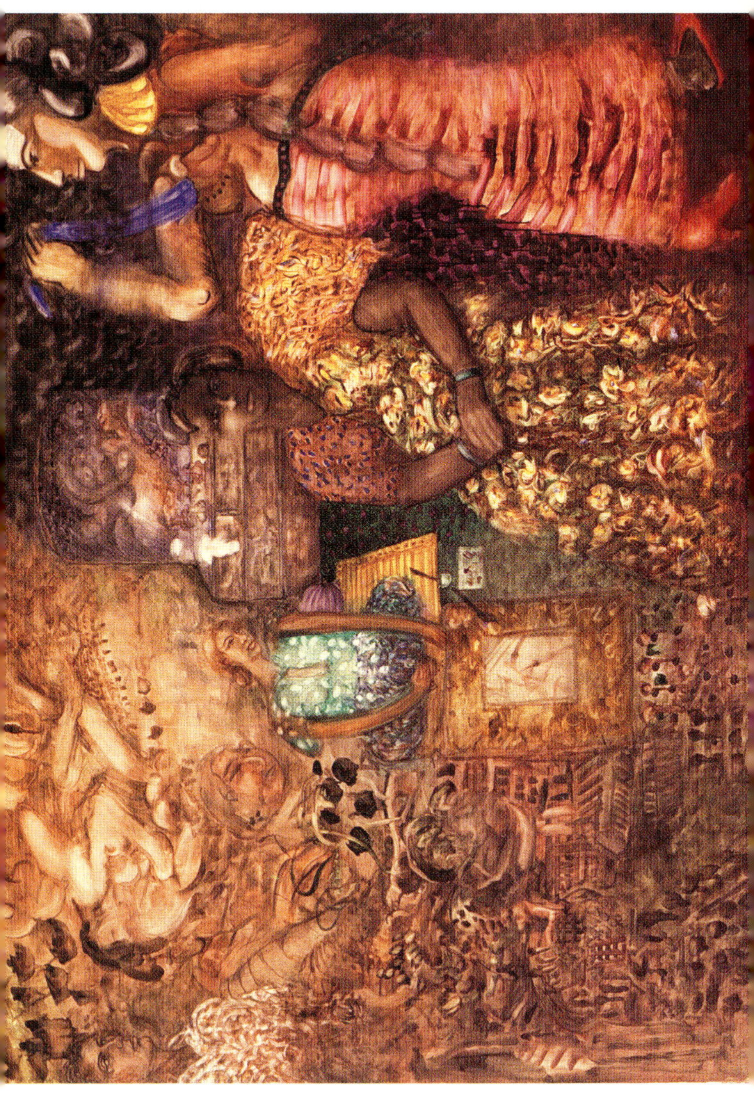

■ Vivan Sundaram, *Arabesque*, 1989

137 x 175 cm, oil on canvas, collection: National Gallery of Modern Art, New Delhi

A painting that weaves intertextual webs with its densely packed images, patterns, and textures. Whether emerging through accumulated strata or dissolving apparition-like into the shadows of memory and time, meanings are glimpsed between the variously styled figures of the three women and the series of social and cultural allusions they engender.

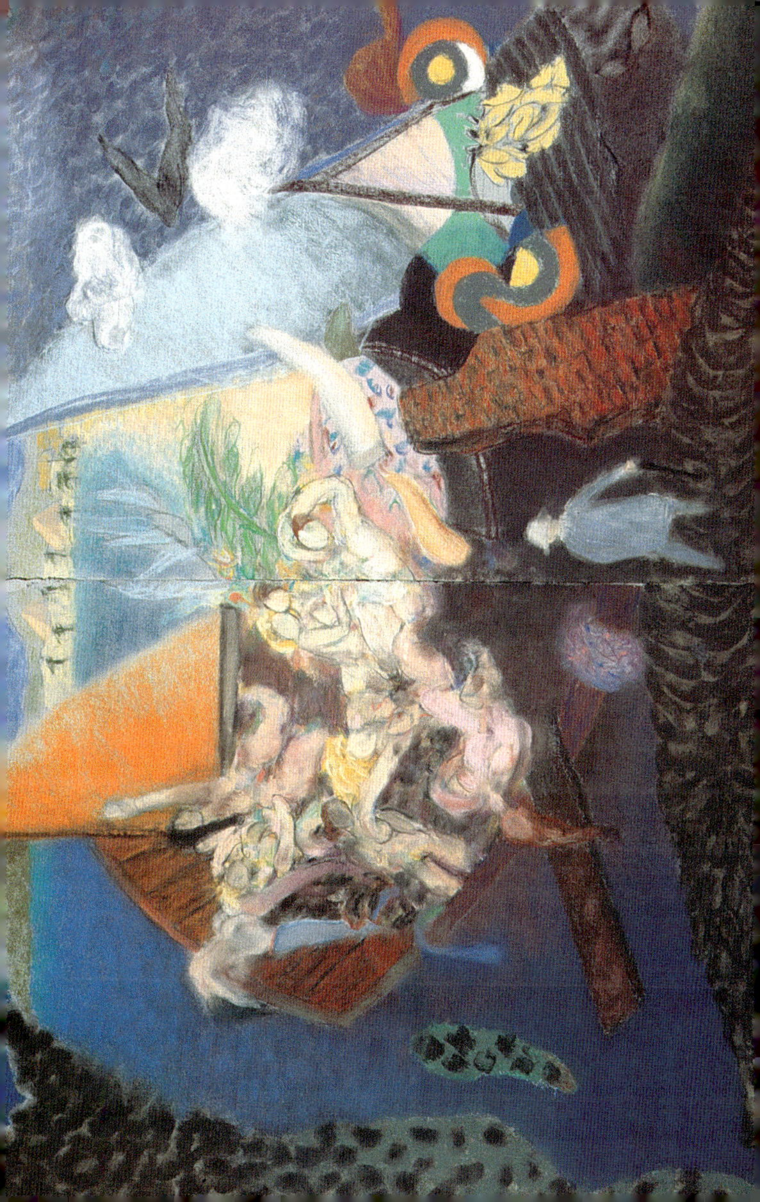

■ Vivan Sundaram, *Orientalist,* 1987

63 x 96 cm, soft pastel on paper, collection: Dhruv and Rati Sawhney, New Delhi

With this depiction (from the exhibition, Journey*) of a just-arrived cargo of female nudes being surveyed by an 'orientalist', the artist seems to be constructing a colonial hypothesis as an instrument of power and exploitation. The work's adjustments of scale and perspective heighten the disjunctiveness of an otherwise lyrical composition, even as its voyeuristic position establishes an uneasy complicity with the viewer.*

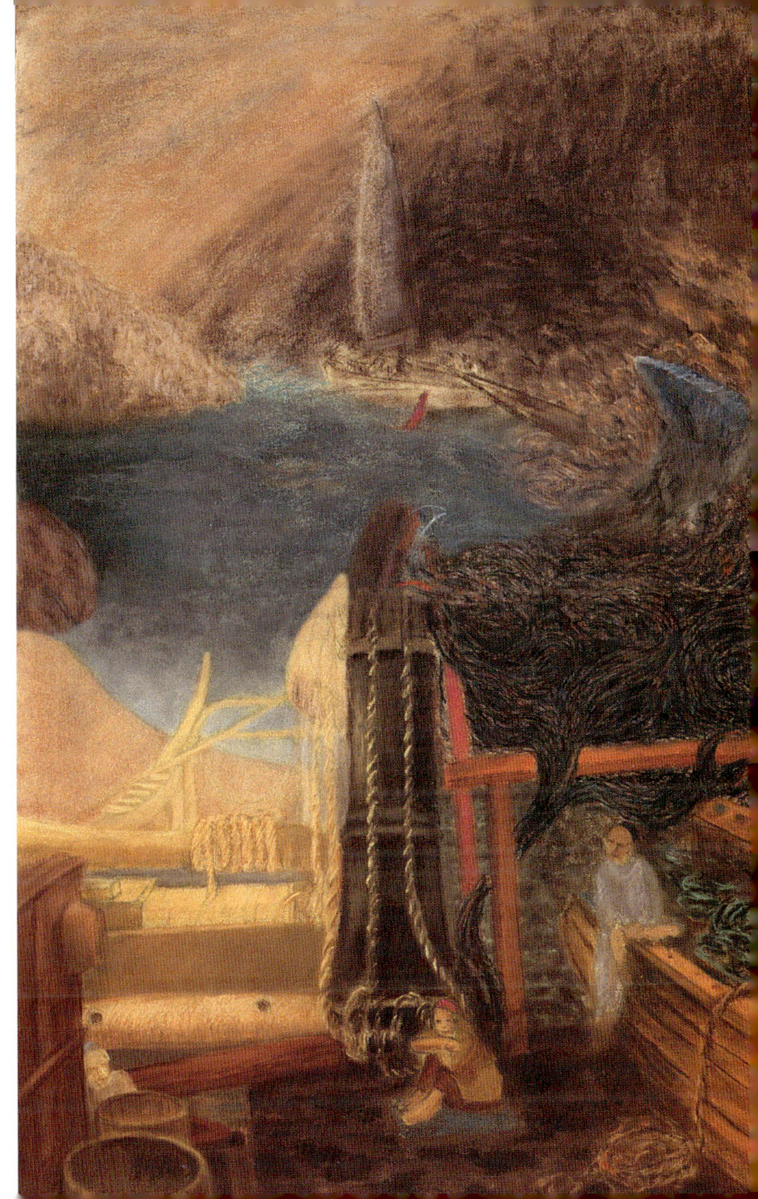

■ Vivan Sundaram, *Chinese Junk with Dreaming Seamen*, 1987

96 x 63 cm, soft pastel on paper, collection: Sara Abraham, Bangalore

The symbolic/narrative logic of this work, with its sensual surfaces, its rubbed and burnished textures, its colours glowing from within, and its range of art historical references, including a Van Gogh-like swirl of ascending strokes, all underscore the process of travel and passage. The series to which it belongs (the exhibition, Journey*) could itself be read as a political and artistic metaphor.*

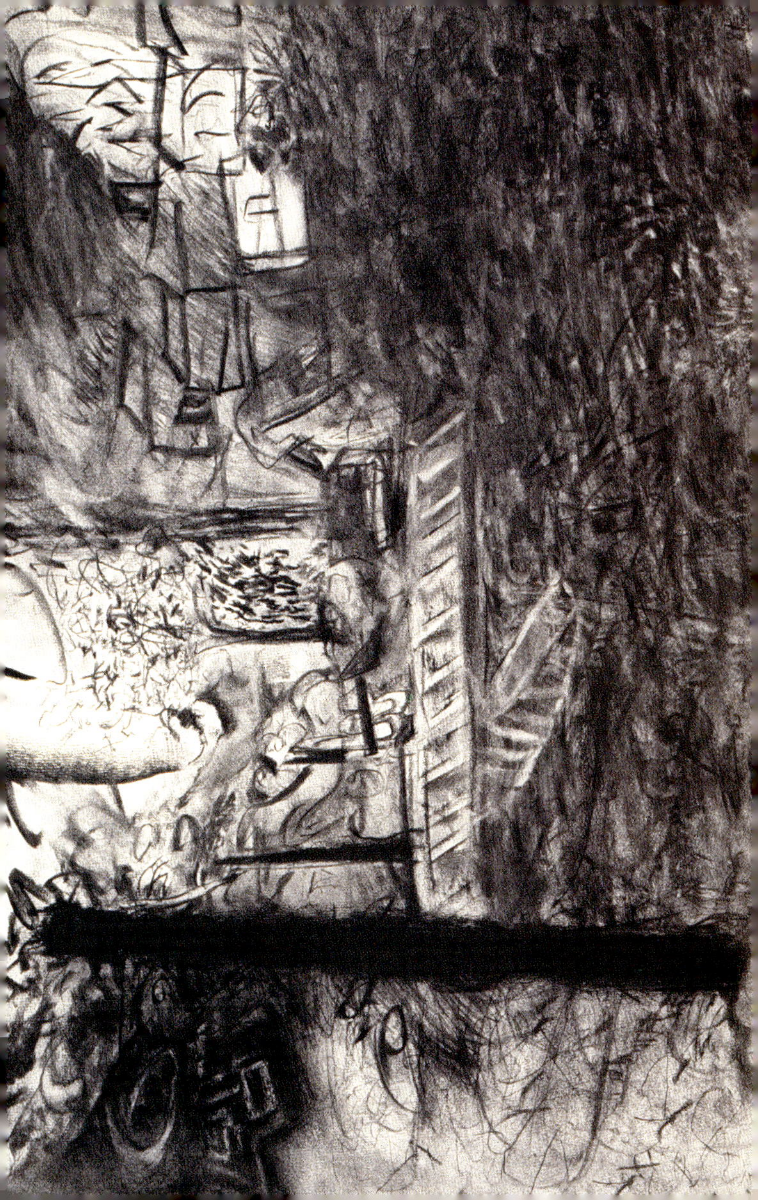

■ Vivan Sundaram, *Entering the Zone*, 1987

70 x 100 cm, charcoal on paper, collection: Artist, New Delhi

The work moves through a surface agitated by a scrim of dense, frenetic marks and half images to a sense of dark foreboding; to involute, elemental forms and their threatening dynamics. 'The passage of white, and the intensity of black, provide so much contrast that what you discover would of necessity be the zone of grey representing a levelling down, the barest, the minimal, which is all your eye and soul can take in.' (Vivan Sundaram)

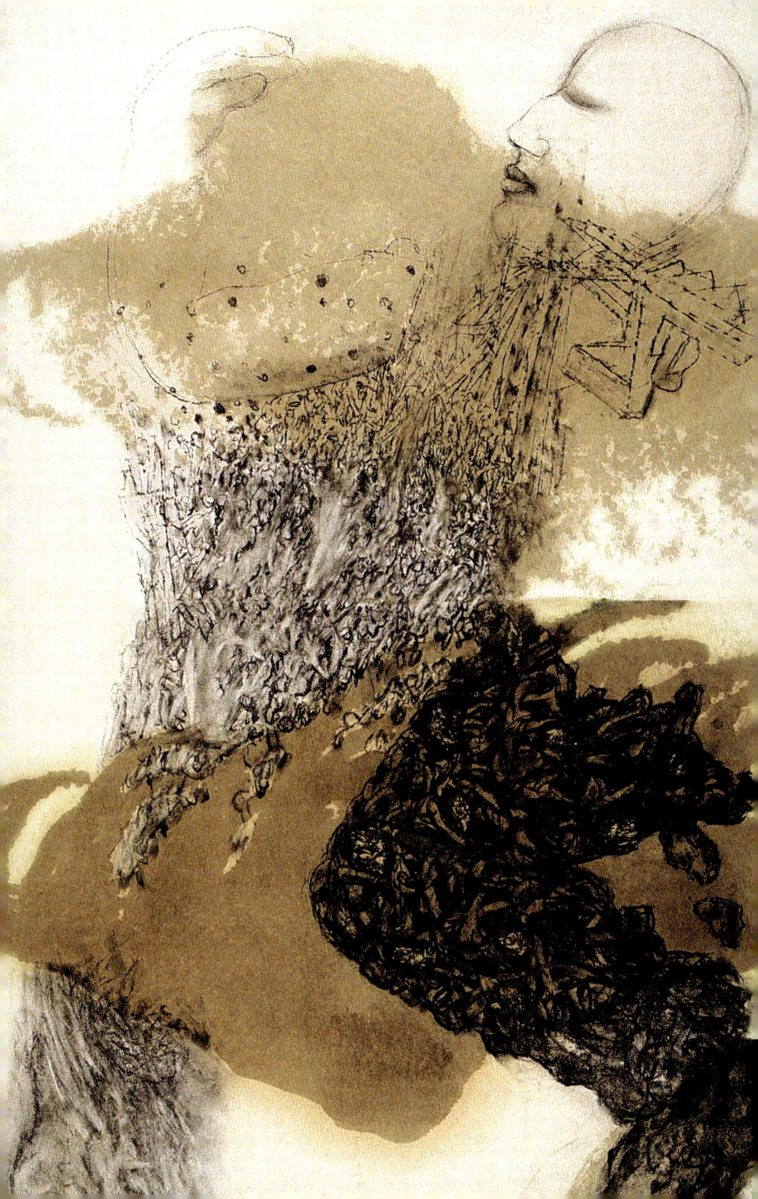

■ Vivan Sundaram, *Soldier of Babylon*, 1991

76 x 112 cm (diptych), engine oil and charcoal on paper, collection: Suresh Jindal, New Delhi

There is a preoccupation with death and catastrophe, themes that recur in the artist's work. 'They propel painful and passionate journeys to other lands, to wars, to carnage on the streets,' says Vivan Sundaram. The dismembered body parts surface momentarily like shadowy hallucinations, only to be absorbed back into the smoke and oil spills of congealed violence.

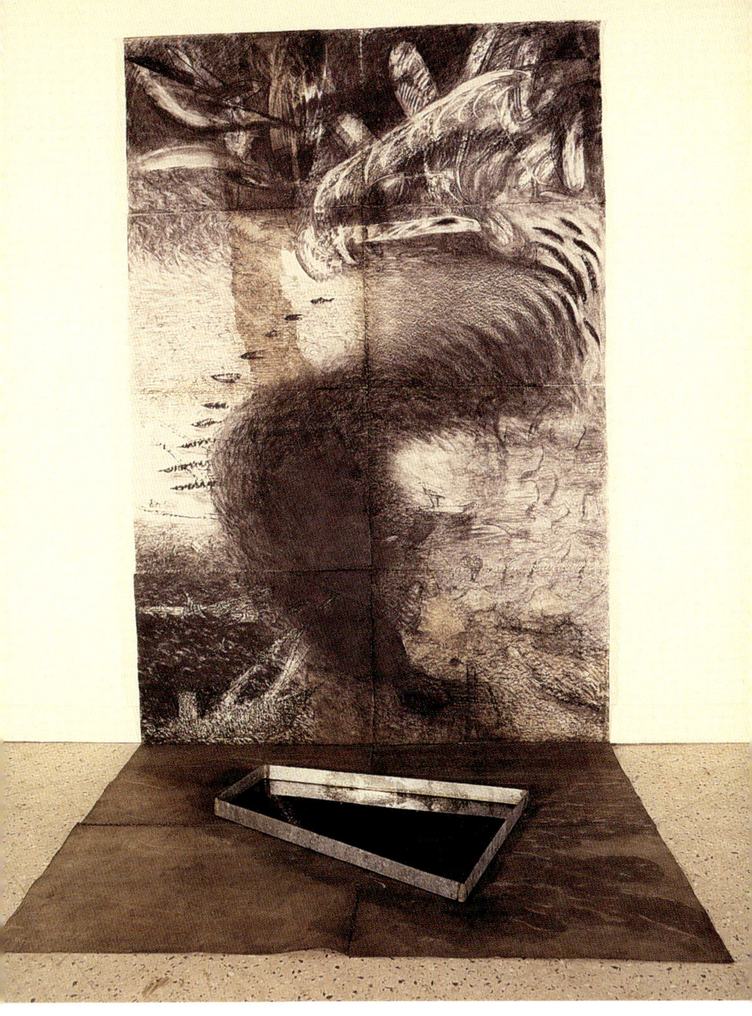

■ Vivan Sundaram, *100,000 Sorties*, 1991

346 x 153 cm, stitched paper on wall and floor with engine oil in zinc tray, collection: Devinder and Kanwaldeep Sawhney, Mumbai

The dark gesture, moody and theatrical; the toxic cloud, continuous, flaring, spiralling upwards in a furious stain, exploding in frenzy, dissipating in conflagrations that disperse in the work's outer margins.

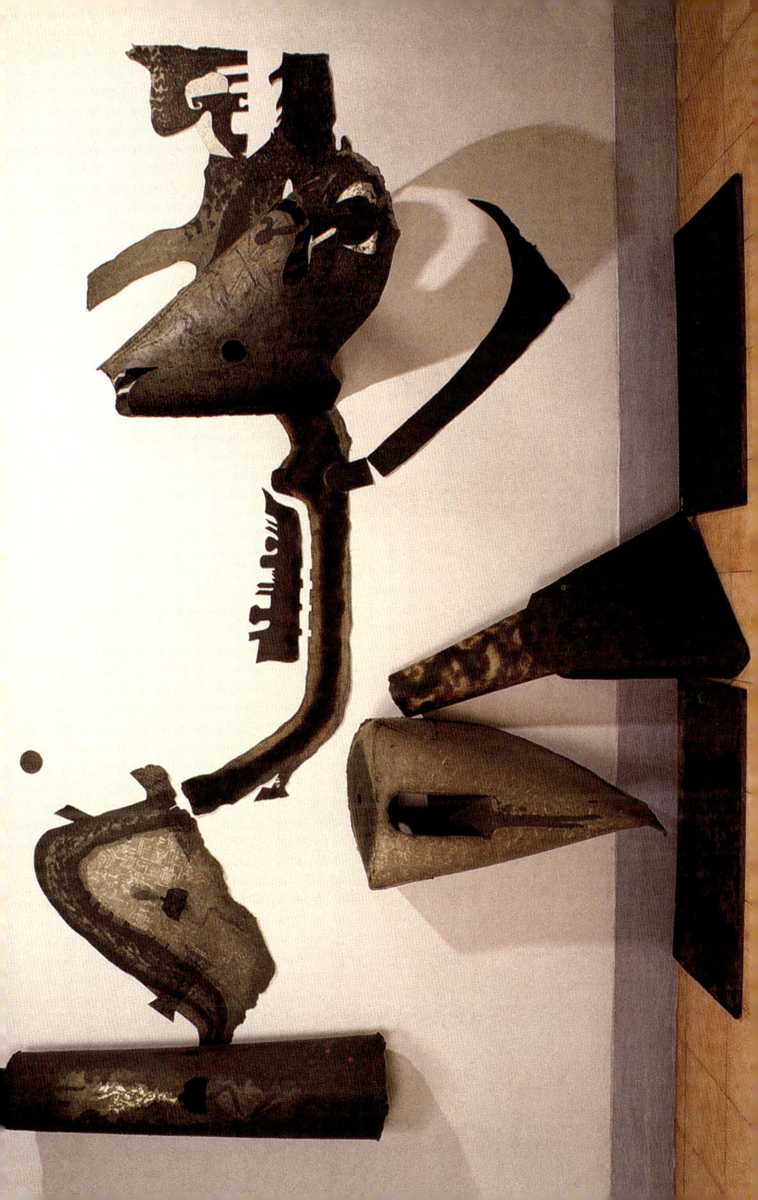

■ Vivan Sundaram, *A River Carries Its Past*, 1992

203 x 305 x 30 cm, engine oil and burn marks on Kalamkhush handmade paper, oil and water in zinc trays, collection: Devinder and Kanwaldeep Sawhney, Mumbai

A part of the Riverscape series, it is a response to an initiative by Cleveland Arts, UK, where the artist conveyed the industrial/commercial intimation of a dockside environment along the banks of the River Tees. The distilled unfolding of this sculptural ensemble's changing evocations is at once mysterious and mythic, suggestive of impermanence and decay.

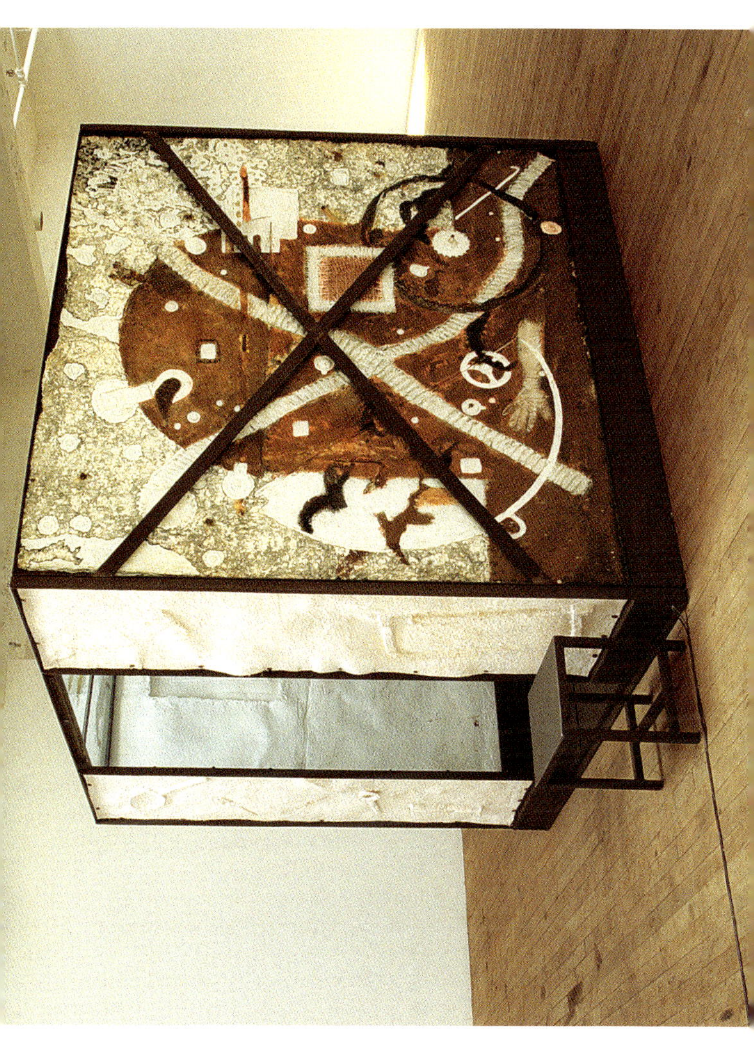

■ Vivan Sundaram, *House/Boat (House: installation view)*, 1994

210 x 210 x 210 cm, Kalamkhush handmade paper, steel, glass, wood, break grease, water, acrylic paint, video, collection: Artist, New Delhi

'The house, in the form of a cube, is white and minimalist. Inside [it] is a black box on which is placed a vessel with water; through the transparent base can be seen the flames of burning furniture in a video loop. On one hand is the reference to monuments/dwellings destroyed, while the other [reference] is that of a home cradling fire and light, with evocations of warmth, food and shelter.' (Vivan Sundaram in an interview for the exhibition, *Shelter,* in 1999 at New Delhi/Mumbai)

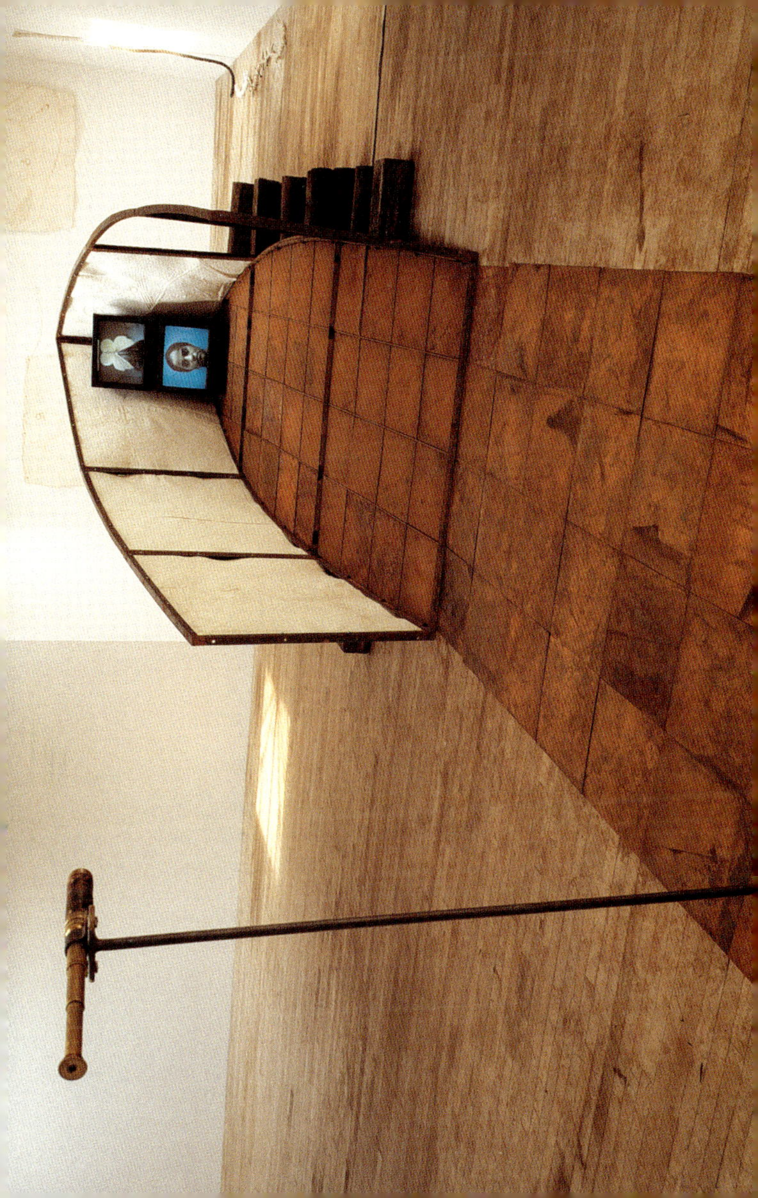

■ Vivan Sundaram, *House/Boat (Boat: installation view)*, 1994

700 x 250 x 180 cm, Kalamkhush handmade paper, steel, glass, wood, video monitor (with Maya Krishna Rao in performance), collection: Artist, New Delhi

---

'The boat, a container grounded for temporary shelter, and stationed beside the assaulted home, is wide open for the spectator to walk into, or to view the video enactment at the prow end. Propped up on railway sleepers, the ensemble can also be read as that of a cross: the dysfunctional boat, hoisted up awkwardly, its body lying on heavy blocks of wood carrying the marks of nails.' (Vivan Sundaram in an interview for the exhibition, *Shelter,* in 1999 at Delhi/Mumbai)

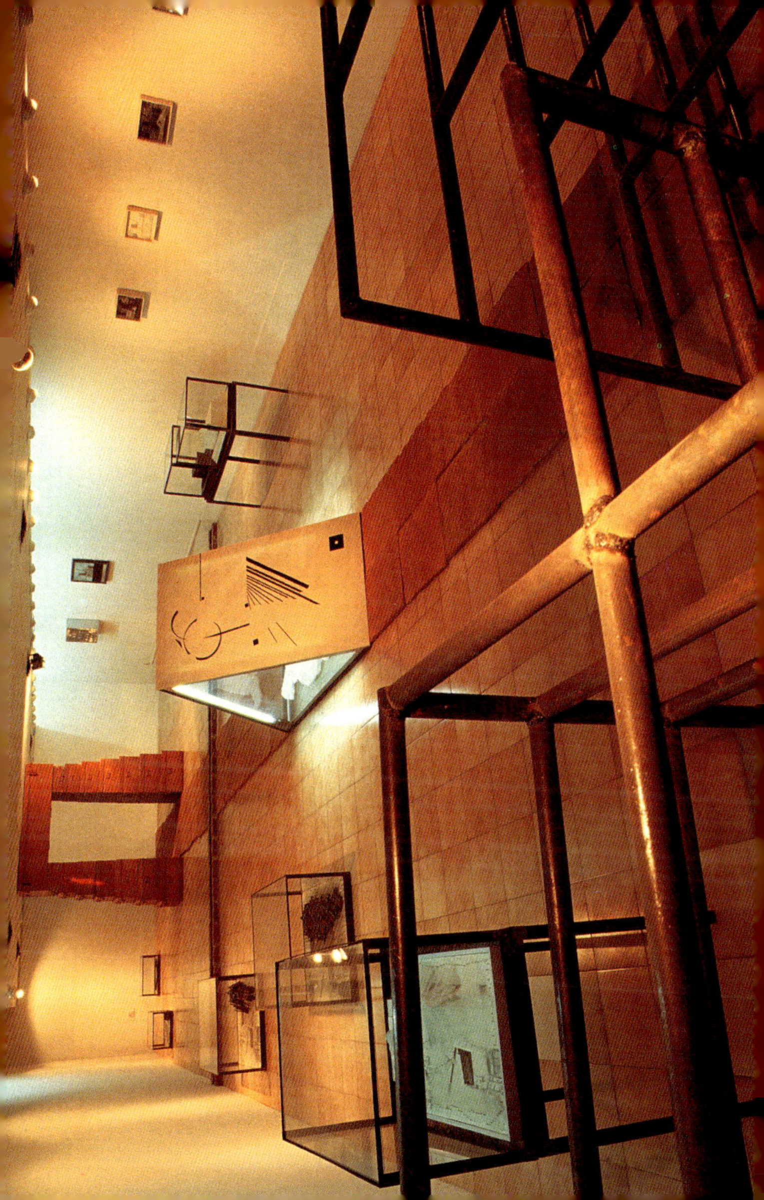

■ Vivan Sundaram, *Memorial (installation view)*, 1993
500 x 1800 cm, New Delhi

The many parts of this large installation, with spaces in between, were connected notionally by the single idea of the '92-'93 communal riots that took place in Mumbai in the aftermath of the demolition of the Babri Masjid. In its different aspects, the work simultaneously mourned and honoured the innocent victims of this carnage.

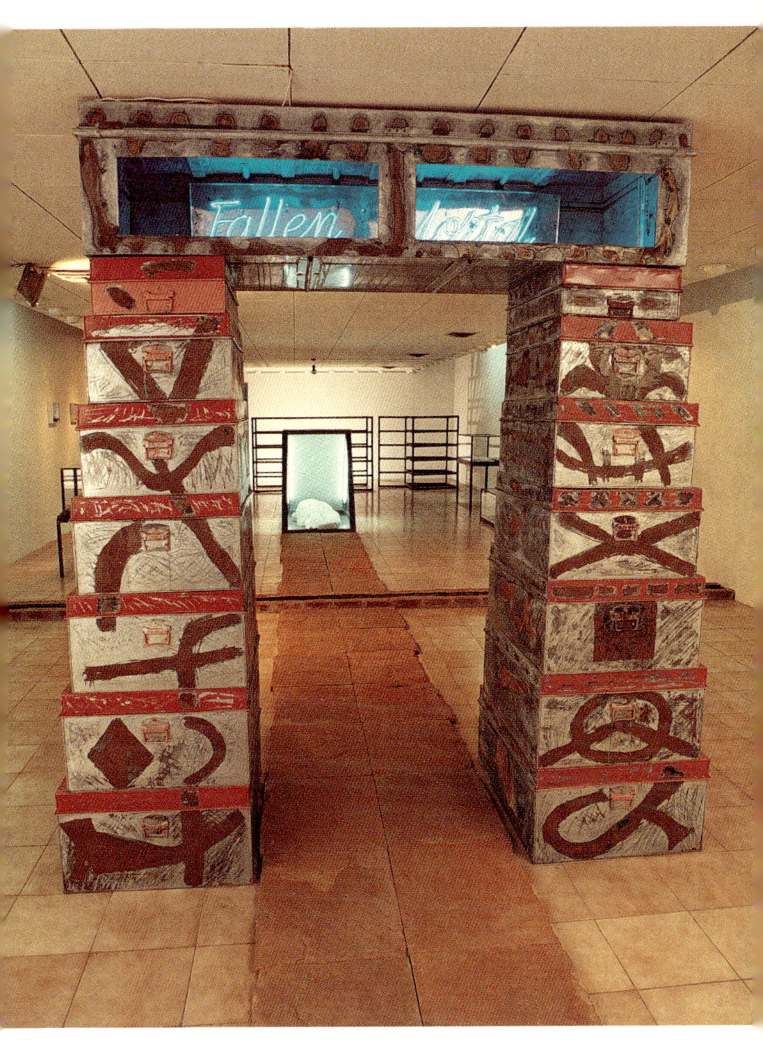
Fallen

■ Vivan Sundaram, *Memorial (Gateway: installation view)*, 1993
231 x 216 x 84 cm, oil, tin, neon, collection: Artist, New Delhi

Ordinary, everyday objects of storage (home) and travel (migration): tin trunks, put together in an unexpected combination, emanate a monumental, hieratic feeling. The work involves a passage: a pathway of red sandstone slabs, intersected by a channel of blood. The walk-through engages the spectator by means of active involvement in a recall of the '92-'93 Mumbai riots, a reminder that some things are never forgotten.

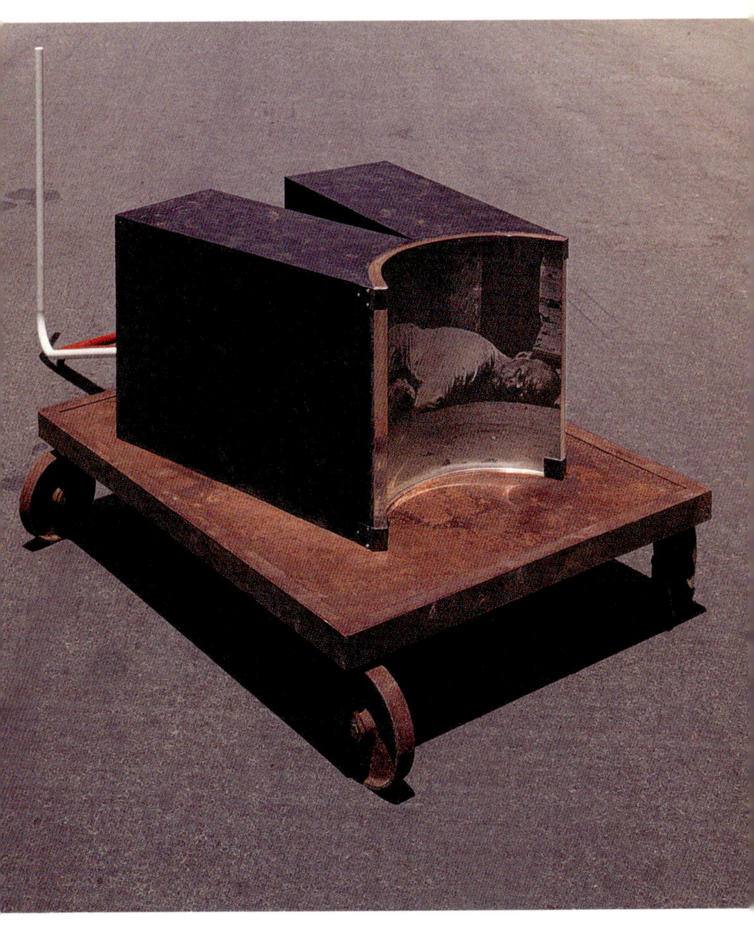

■ Vivan Sundaram, *Gun Carriage*, 1995 (remade 2000)

106 x 292 x 104 cm, acrylic sheet, detail of photograph by Hoshi Jal, The Times of India, Mumbai, collection: Artist, New Delhi

The photographic image of an anonymous victim of the '92-'93 Mumbai riots is enshrined/compacted in a box that resembles the metal container on the road seen in the original news photograph. Mounted on an everyday municipal trolley, the split-open configuration can also be interpreted as a compressed coffin. Serious irony underlies the allegorical/documentary mode of this sculpture that enjoins the viewer to contemplate the death of a person, and that of humanity itself.

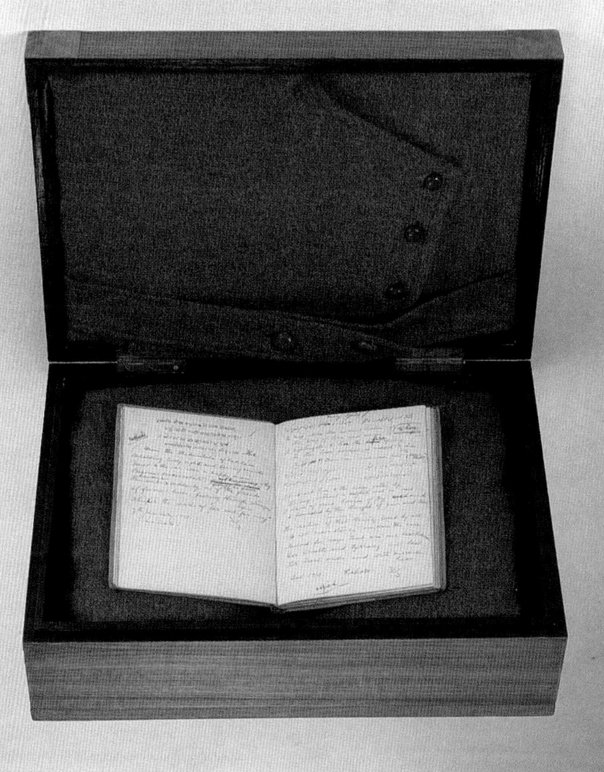

■ Vivan Sundaram, *The Sher-Gil Archive (Box one: Father)*, 1995

12 x 50 x 34 cm, teak board, woollen cloth, paper, collection: Queensland Art Gallery, Brisbane

The box with its reconstruction of historical traces, of personal objects, and articles of clothing, becomes as it were a reliquary, holding evocations of life, as well as of fiction, that must linger somewhere behind the facade of documentary detachment.

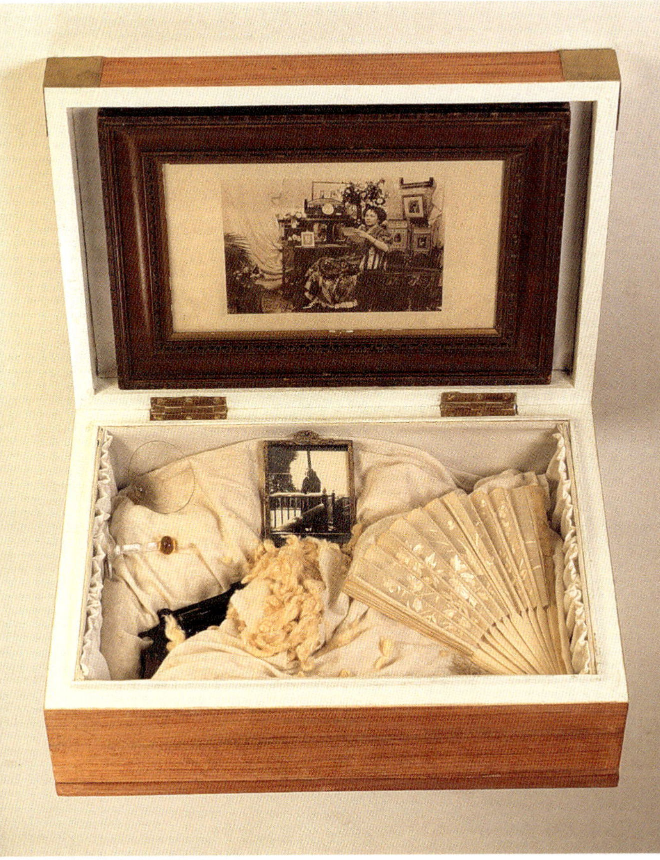

■ Vivan Sundaram, *The Sher-Gil Archive (Box two: Mother)*, 1995

12 x 50 x 34 cm, teak board, silk, glass, cotton, wool, metal, photograph, collection: Nitin Bhayana, New Delhi

The articles, all personal possessions, seem to define themselves in a sphere outside their materiality. This makes for a subtle interplay of emotional elements that recalls, as if through mists of time, the long-departed presence and social milieu of the original owner.

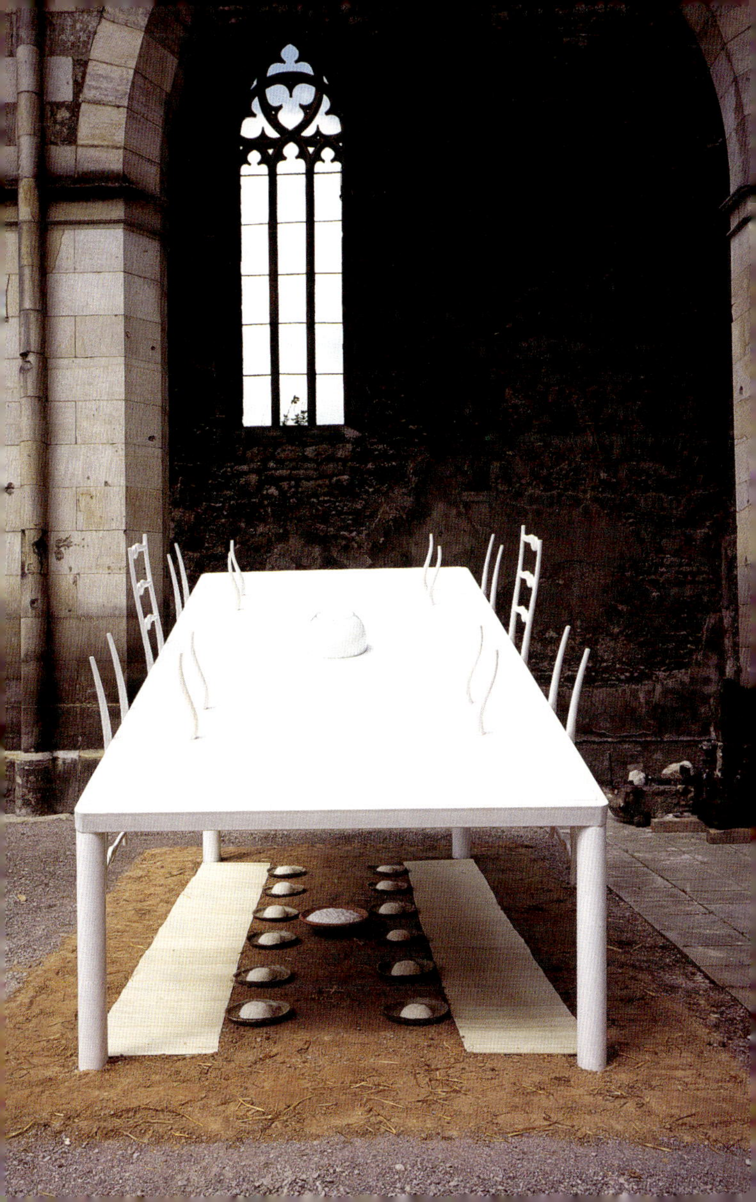

■ Vivan Sundaram, *The Table is Laid*, 1995

200 x 200 x 400 cm, wood, terracotta, glass, straw, rice, and curd, collection: Artist, New Delhi

The odd transformation of commonplace objects – a sloping tabletop, tilting chairs, food served under the table instead of on top – all energise the sculptural installation, serving to intensify its metaphoric disjunctures: the concepts of community, shelter and sustenance, worked through reflective viewing.

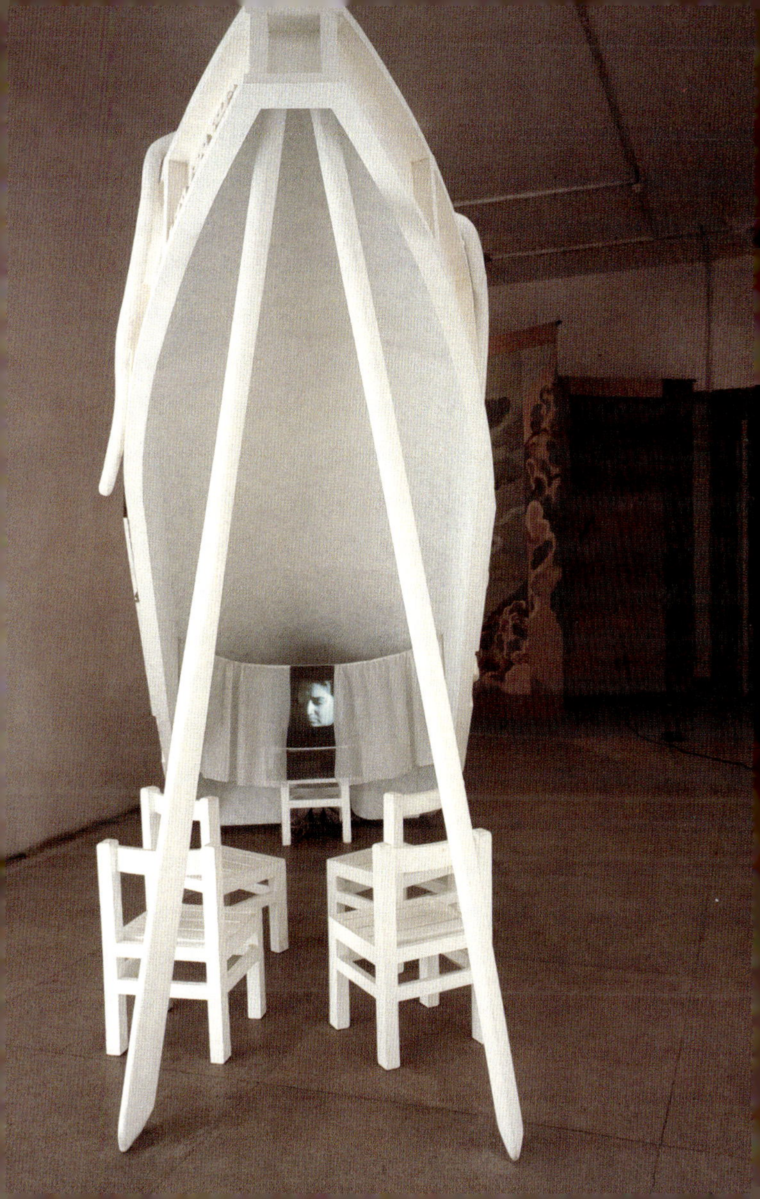

■ Vivan Sundaram, *Carrier*, 1996

225 x 125 x 400 cm, wood, acrylic, paint cloth, video monitor (Shubha Mudgal in performance), collection: Artist, New Delhi

---

'The beached boat marks the culmination of many voyages. As an archaeological find, it has been salvaged from the depths of a dark ocean, to lie inverted and propped up on its oars. Its interior is pure white space – a shrine, a place for congregation. The woman, her face luminous on the monitor, sings of journeys and longings in the Sufi/Bhakti (devotional) *tradition[s]. She inhabits a space that defies possession.'* (Vivan Sundaram's statement in the catalogue of the Second Asia-Pacific Triennial, Brisbane, 1996)

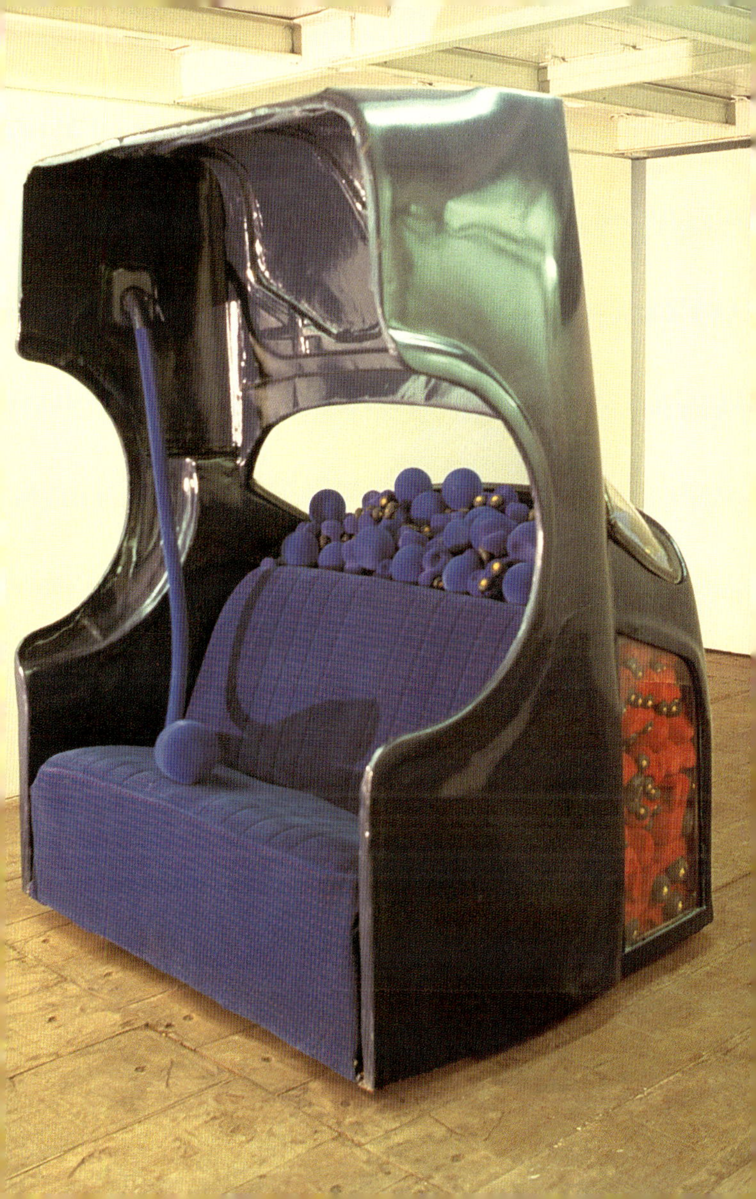

■ Vivan Sundaram, *Kar-Khel*, 2000

180 x 122 x 122 cm, Metal, glass, latex, floc, cloth, collection: Artist, New Delhi

Incongruity is built into a work that plays on differences. An Oxford blue, high-gloss car has been sharply bisected, but its seat, soft and plush, remains intact. One can sit on it, or play with the hybrid, brightly coloured toys that spill out of every conceivable niche. Questions of function and consumption, and their subversion, get thrown up in a work that is positioned like a riddle between perceptual experience and meaning.

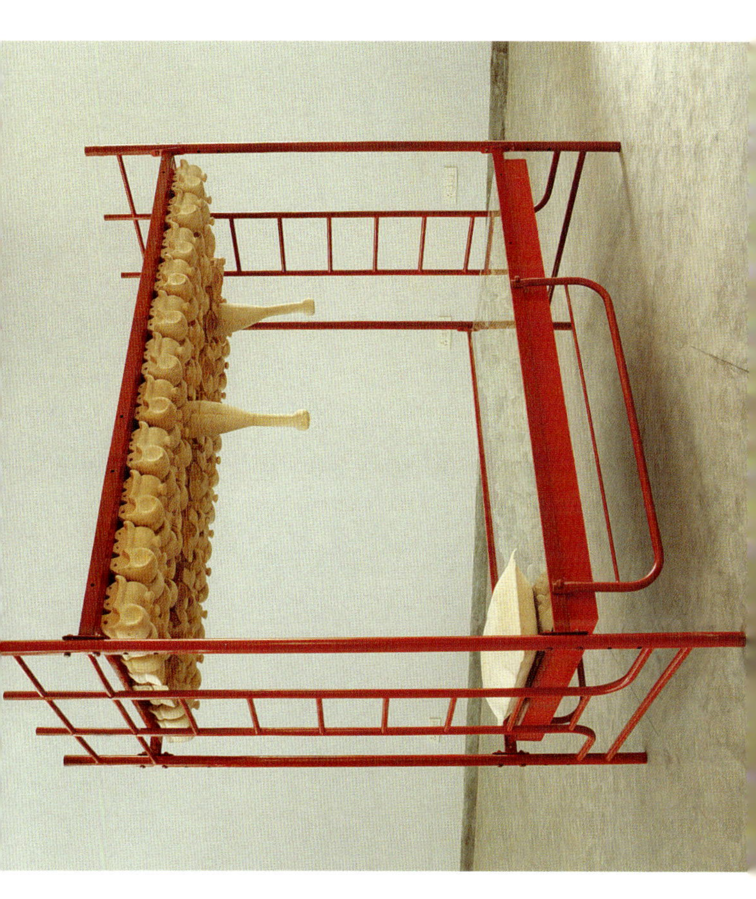

- Vivan Sundaram, *Bunk Bed*, 1999

  200 x 122 x 245 cm, enamel, paint, steel, latex, glass, collection: Artist, New Delhi

  The conventional bunk bed, though turned upside down, evokes the elements of shelter, of a house, of a child's memory of security, comfort, warmth, and repose. But the toy-filled mattresses, playgrounds of tactile, visual experiences, suspended out of reach or trapped behind glass, suggest the melancholia of a time and age that can never be retrieved.

- *Front cover:* Vivan Sundaram, *Quintal of Grass*, 1985

  168 x 112 cm, oil on canvas, collection: Prema Srinivasan, Chennai

  Often figures in the paintings of the mid-80s had a still, enervated quality while the depiction of backgrounds and objects was more active and sensuous. Gestural brush marks worked at the level of sensations and became indicators of meaning. Here, the energised sheaf of grass that flares up into the sky, gives definition to the man; 'it has the potential to liberate him; he can fly like Icarus, or like him be destroyed.'

- *Page 2:* Vivan Sundaram
- *Page 3:* Vivan Sundaram, *The Sher-Gil Archive (Boxfive : Family Album)*, 1995

  12 x 50 x 34 cm, teak board, acrylic sheet, mirror, cloth, water, collection: Czaee Shah, Mumbai